EARTHQUAKES

Jennifer Nault

www.av2books.com

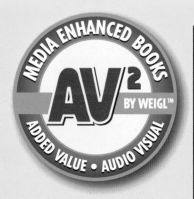

MEDIA ENHANCED BOOKS
AV² BY WEIGL™
ADDED VALUE • AUDIO VISUAL

Go to **www.av2books.com**, and enter this book's unique code.

BOOK CODE

Q 6 0 9 5 9 5

AV² by Weigl brings you media enhanced books that support active learning.

AV² provides enriched content that supplements and complements this book. Weigl's AV² books strive to create inspired learning and engage young minds in a total learning experience.

Your AV² Media Enhanced books come alive with...

Audio
Listen to sections of the book read aloud.

Key Words
Study vocabulary, and complete a matching word activity.

Video
Watch informative video clips.

Quizzes
Test your knowledge.

Embedded Weblinks
Gain additional information for research.

Slide Show
View images and captions, and prepare a presentation.

Try This!
Complete activities and hands-on experiments.

... and much, much more!

Published by AV² by Weigl
350 5th Avenue, 59th Floor
New York, NY 10118
Website: www.av2books.com   www.weigl.com

Library of Congress Cataloging-in-Publication Data

Nault, Jennifer.
 Earthquakes / Jennifer Nault.
   p. cm. -- (Earth science)
Includes index.
 ISBN 978-1-60596-964-0 (hardcover : alk. paper) -- ISBN 978-1-60596-965-7 (softcover : alk. paper) -- ISBN 978-1-60596-966-4 (e-book)
1. Earthquakes--Juvenile literature. I. Title.
 QE521.3.N383 2010
 551.22--dc22
                    2009050958

Printed in the United States of America in North Mankato, Minnesota
2 3 4 5 6 7 8 9 0 15 14 13 12 11

082011
WEP170811

Project Coordinator Heather C. Hudak
Design Terry Paulhus

Photo Credits
Every reasonable effort has been made to trace ownership and to obtain permission to reprint copyright material. The publishers would be pleased to have any errors or omissions brought to their attention so that they may be corrected in subsequent printings.

Weigl acknowledges Getty Images as its primary image supplier for this title.

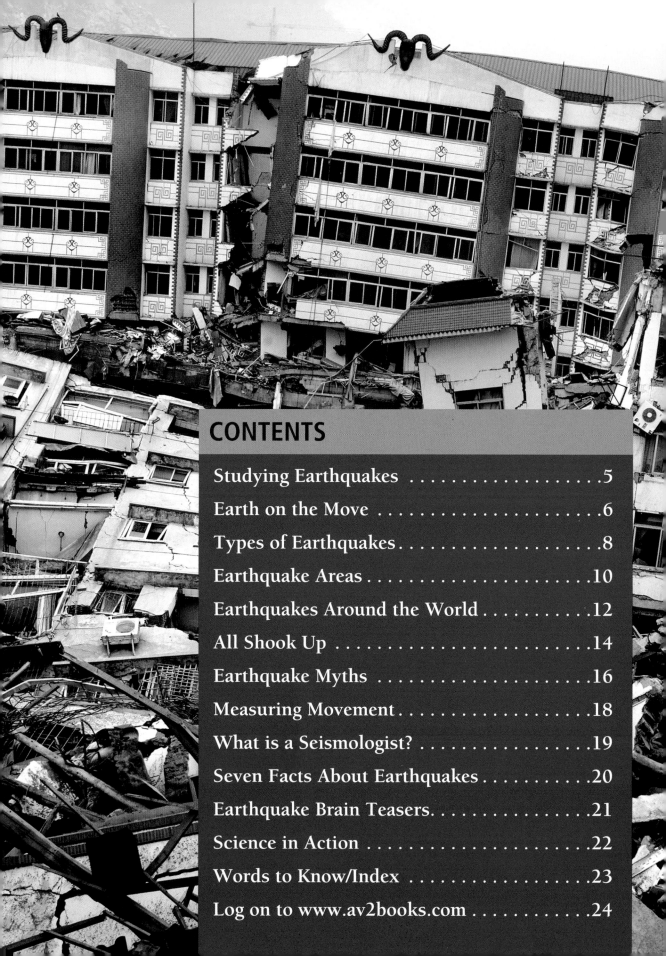

CONTENTS

Until recently, it was thought that all earthquakes had been caused by natural processes. Scientists have found, however, that human activities can help cause earthquakes. Activities such as mining, oil drilling, and building dams can shift where large amounts of weight sit on Earth's **crust**. In 2008, a very large dam built in China may have helped cause an earthquake in the Sichuan region. Nearly 80,000 people were missing or killed during this earthquake.

Studying Earthquakes

Shaking or trembling of the ground is an earthquake. Earthquakes occur when rocks along a crack in Earth's surface suddenly shift. The earthquake releases stress that has slowly built up in the rocks. Earthquakes can leave long cracks in the ground. The ground can appear as though it has split in two.

Most earthquakes are too small for people to feel. Some earthquakes are bigger. A few cause great damage. Earthquakes have killed thousands of people. They can cause buildings to fall, roads to crack, and water dams to burst. Earthquakes cannot be prevented. People did not understand how earthquakes happened until the early 20th century. Today, scientists study earthquakes. They **predict** where future earthquakes may occur.

■ An earthquake occurs someplace in the world every 30 seconds. Most are too small to cause damage.

Earth on the Move

Earth's surface is always moving. Earth's crust is broken into tectonic plates. These are large pieces of crust that shift and move. They are always joining together and pulling apart. When tectonic plates move, the edges grate or scrape against each other. This movement causes Earth to tremble. The place where tectonic plates meet is called a fault line. Fault lines can be 1 inch (2.5 centimeters) or many miles (kilometers) long. They may also be vertical, horizontal, or slanted at an angle.

When tectonic plates rub against each other, they create pressure. Over time, the pressure builds. The pressure may build over many years.

TYPES OF FAULTS

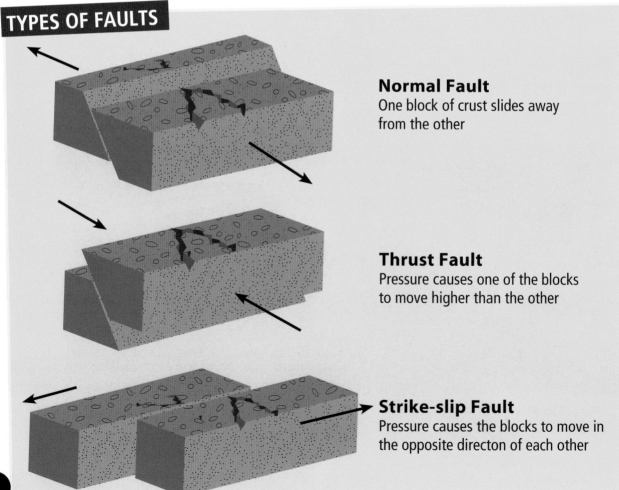

Normal Fault
One block of crust slides away from the other

Thrust Fault
Pressure causes one of the blocks to move higher than the other

Strike-slip Fault
Pressure causes the blocks to move in the opposite directon of each other

When the pressure grows too strong, the plates suddenly move. The pressure is released. Shock waves move through Earth's crust. They cause the ground to shake and tremble. This is an earthquake.

EARTHQUAKE CLOSE-UP

What does an earthquake look like from inside Earth? Scientists have studied earthquakes for many years. They have learned how an earthquake happens and what it looks like.

The place where energy is first released is called the focus. The focus can be near Earth's surface. The closer the focus is to the surface, the more damage the earthquake will cause. The earthquake begins on Earth's surface above the focus. This spot is called the epicenter. Here, the shock waves are strongest. The epicenter is usually where the most damage occurs.

Epicenter
The epicenter is the spot on Earth's surface that is above the focus.

Fault scarp
A fault scarp is a steep slope on Earth's surface that results from fault movement.

Fault trace
A fault trace is the line showing the fault on Earth's surface.

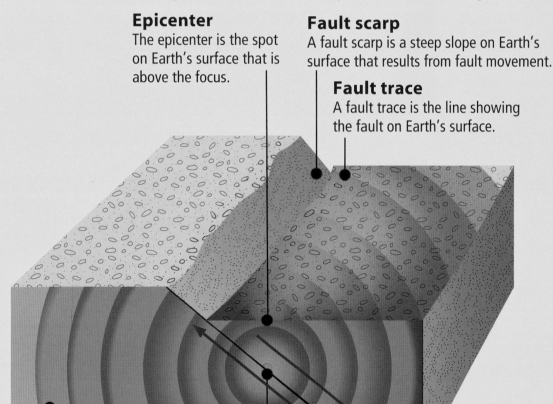

Shock waves
Shock waves cause the ground to shake. Some travel inside the Earth while others travel along the surface.

Focus
The focus is the point inside Earth where the earthquake begins.

Fault plane
The fault plane is the place where rock on one side of a fracture has moved in relation to rock on the other side of the fracture.

Types of Earthquakes

Some earthquakes are very powerful. Others can hardly be felt. Dr. Charles Richter created a way to measure earthquakes in 1935. The Richter scale measures the height of **seismic waves**.

MAGNITUDE 1

- Cannot be felt on the surface

MAGNITUDE 2

- Can only be felt slightly near the epicenter

MAGNITUDE 3

- Can be felt near the epicenter, but causes little damage

The scale gives number values to the amount of energy created during an earthquake. The number linked to an earthquake is called its **magnitude**.

MAGNITUDE 4–5

- Can cause damage in small areas and is felt about 20 miles (32 kilometers) away

MAGNITUDE 6

- Can be felt over a large area and can cause much more damage

MAGNITUDE 7–8

- Can cause buildings to fall and people to die
- Widespread **destruction**

Earthquake Areas

Earthquakes can happen at any time. They can strike anywhere in the world. Most earthquakes happen along the edges of tectonic plates. Usually, this is near the edges of **continents**.

There are two main areas where earthquakes occur. One is called the circum-Pacific belt. It circles the Pacific Ocean. This area includes the western coasts of Japan, North and South America, and the Philippines. The other area is called the Alpide belt. It cuts through Europe and Asia.

Japan experiences the most earthquakes in the world. Ten percent of all earthquakes occur in Japan. However, earthquakes have caused great damage around the world.

■ Most earthquakes in the United States take place in Alaska. As many as 4,000 are recorded in Alaska each year.

Earthquake Timeline

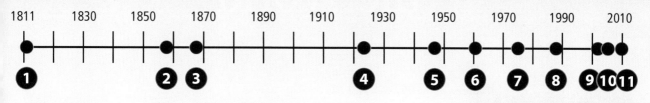

1811 1830 1850 1870 1890 1910 1930 1950 1970 1990 2010

1 **2** **3** **4** **5** **6** **7** **8** **9** **10** **11**

1 ## 1811
Three earthquakes between December 1811 and February 1812 hit New Madrid, Missouri. Each quake was estimated to be close to a magnitude of 8 on the Richter scale.

2 ## 1857
Fort Tejon, California, is hit by an estimated magnitude 7.9 earthquake. The earthquake is felt over more than 135,000 square miles (350,000 square kilometers) of land.

3 ## 1868
Hawai'ian volcano Mauna Loa erupts, creating an earthquake of magnitude 7.9.

4 ## 1923
The Great Kanto earthquake happens in Japan. It measures 8.3 on the Richter scale and has its focus underwater. The earthquake, along with the resulting **tsunami**, kills more than 100,000 people.

5 ## 1948
The Soviet province of Turkmenistan has a massive earthquake. This 7.3-magnitude quake kills nearly 110,000 people.

6 ## 1960
The largest recorded earthquake, measuring 9.5, strikes Santiago, Chile. The quake causes a tsunami that hits Japan, Hawai'i, and the Philippines. Nearly 2,000 people are killed.

7 ## 1976
An estimated 240,000 people die during two earthquakes in Tangshan, China. The first quake has a magnitude of 7.5. A second, smaller quake happens 15 hours later.

8 ## 1988
An earthquake of 6.8 on the Richter scale shakes Armenia. About 45,000 people are killed. In some towns, almost all of the buildings fall.

9 ## 2004
A magnitude 9.0 earthquake in the Indian Ocean causes a tsunami. This tsunami strikes several Asian countries and kills between 150,000 and 275,000 people.

10 ## 2005
A magnitude 7.6 earthquake strikes the Kashmir region of Pakistan, killing at least 86,000 people.

11 ## 2010
A massive earthquake takes place in Haiti. Hundreds of thousands of people are killed. It is the worst earthquake to happen in the country in 150 years.

Earthquakes Around the World

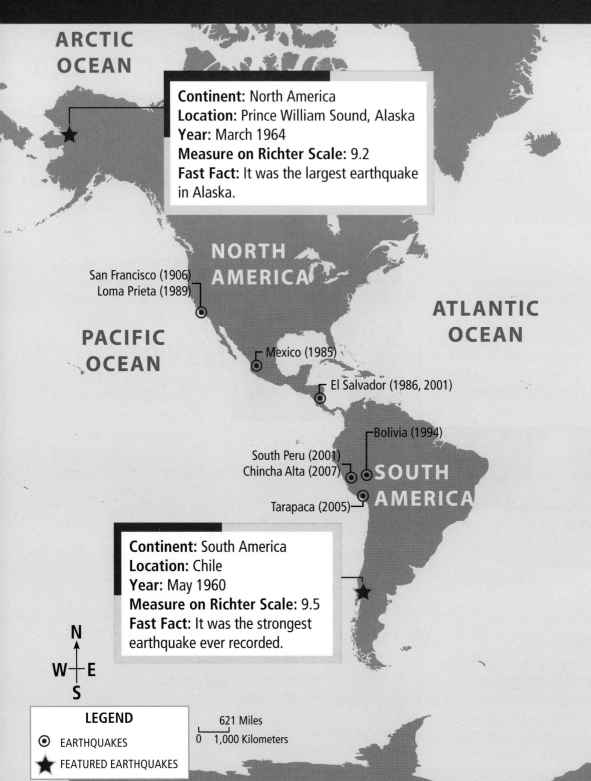

ARCTIC
OCEAN

Continent: North America
Location: Prince William Sound, Alaska
Year: March 1964
Measure on Richter Scale: 9.2
Fast Fact: It was the largest earthquake in Alaska.

NORTH AMERICA

San Francisco (1906)
Loma Prieta (1989)

PACIFIC
OCEAN

ATLANTIC
OCEAN

Mexico (1985)

El Salvador (1986, 2001)

Bolivia (1994)

South Peru (2001)
Chincha Alta (2007)

SOUTH AMERICA

Tarapaca (2005)

Continent: South America
Location: Chile
Year: May 1960
Measure on Richter Scale: 9.5
Fast Fact: It was the strongest earthquake ever recorded.

N
W — E
S

LEGEND

⊙ EARTHQUAKES

★ FEATURED EARTHQUAKES

621 Miles
0   1,000 Kilometers

WHAT HAVE YOU LEARNED ABOUT EARTHQUAKES?

This map shows the locations of some of the major earthquakes that have occurred around the world. Use this map, and research online to answer these questions.

1. Which continent has the most earthquakes?
2. Why do earthquakes occur in these areas?

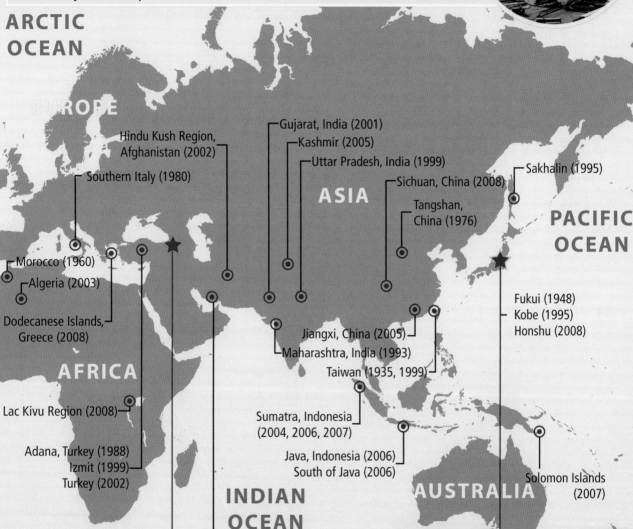

ARCTIC OCEAN

EUROPE

ASIA

PACIFIC OCEAN

AFRICA

INDIAN OCEAN

AUSTRALIA

SOUTHERN OCEAN

ANTARCTICA

Hindu Kush Region, Afghanistan (2002)

Gujarat, India (2001)

Kashmir (2005)

Uttar Pradesh, India (1999)

Sakhalin (1995)

Southern Italy (1980)

Sichuan, China (2008)

Tangshan, China (1976)

Morocco (1960)

Algeria (2003)

Dodecanese Islands, Greece (2008)

Fukui (1948)
Kobe (1995)
Honshu (2008)

Jiangxi, China (2005)

Maharashtra, India (1993)

Taiwan (1935, 1999)

Lac Kivu Region (2008)

Sumatra, Indonesia (2004, 2006, 2007)

Adana, Turkey (1988)
Izmit (1999)
Turkey (2002)

Java, Indonesia (2006)
South of Java (2006)

Solomon Islands (2007)

Bam, SE Iran (2003)
Zarand, Iran (2005)

Continent: Asia/Europe
Location: Armenia
Year: December 1988
Measure on Richter Scale: 6.8
Fast Fact: Between 25,000 and as many as 45,000 people were killed.

Continent: Asia
Location: Japan
Year: September 1923
Measure on Richter Scale: 7.9
Fast Fact: The earthquake's focus was under the sea. This caused a huge tsunami.

All Shook Up

Many earthquakes shake the state of California. The San Andreas Fault is a large fault line. It runs more than 680 miles (1,100 km) through California. It is common for earthquakes to happen along this fault line.

In 1906, a large earthquake struck San Francisco. It measured 8.3 on the Richter scale. Few of San Francisco's buildings were designed to withstand earthquakes. Buildings crashed to the ground. Many people were killed. The earthquake also started a terrible fire, which burned through the city. The fire may have caused even more damage than the earthquake of years ago.

▨ The San Andreas Fault is a strike-slip fault.

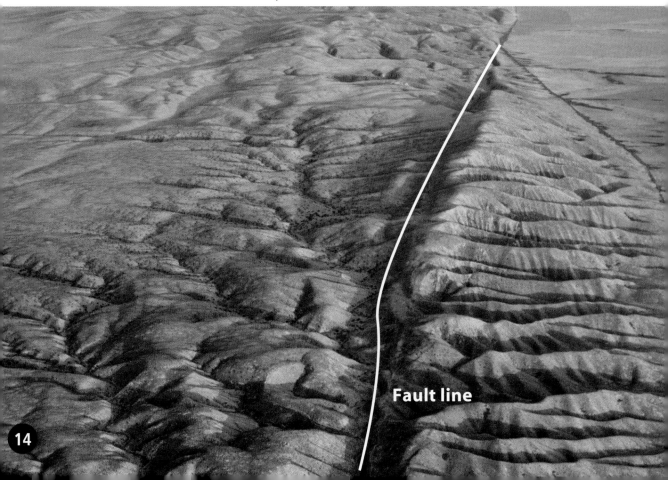

Fault line

People who live in earthquake areas can protect themselves. People can practice how to **evacuate** a building safely. They can learn where to find safe places to wait for an earthquake to stop.

Certain types of buildings can help protect people during earthquakes. Buildings that stand on solid rock are safer than those built on soft ground. Wooden buildings are also safer than brick or stone buildings. The Transamerica Building in San Francisco has a flexible **foundation**. It can sway back and forth during an earthquake without breaking apart or falling down.

EARTHQUAKE SAFETY TIPS

- To prepare for an earthquake, bolt large pieces of furniture to the walls or floor.
- Never place heavy objects, such as large paintings, over a bed. They could fall on a person who is sleeping. If you are in bed when an earthquake occurs, gently roll off the bed to the floor.
- If you are indoors, curl up under a table or a desk.
- Stay far away from mirrors and glass, such as windows.
- If you are in a vehicle, drive to a safe place that is far from concrete overpasses. Remain inside the vehicle.
- If you are outdoors, keep away from power lines, buildings, and trees.
- Never take cover under a stairwell. Stairways may collapse or become unsafe during an earthquake.
- Stay off elevators.

Earthquake Myths

Cultures all over the world have earthquake myths. Hindus thought eight huge elephants held Earth up. Sometimes, an elephant would grow tired. It would shake its head to wake up. This caused Earth to vibrate. Some people believed there were only four elephants. They balanced on the back of a turtle that balanced on the back of a cobra. The ground would shake when any one of these animals moved.

In Japan, some people believed that a giant catfish named Namazu kept the ground floating on top of the sea. When the fish moved, the ground shook. Others believed that Nazamu lived underground. The Kashima god was responsible for keeping Japan safe from earthquakes. He kept Nazamu from moving by placing a rock with special powers on top of him. Sometimes, the Kashima god would be distracted. When this happened, Nazamu would thrash his body, causing earthquakes.

■ Some people believe that animals, such as wolves, can sense when an earthquake is coming. However, this "sense" has never been scientifically proven.

California's Gabrielino Indians believed the Great Spirit created a beautiful place with lakes and rivers. Six large turtles carried this place on their backs. One day, the turtles began to fight. Three of the turtles swam east. At the same time, the others swam west. This caused Earth to vibrate and crack. The land on the turtles' backs was too heavy. They could not swim far. They stopped fighting. Gabrielino Indians thought earthquakes were caused when the turtles would fight again.

Some African cultures believed that Earth sat on top of a giant's head. His hair was made from trees and plants. Animals and people were insects that crawled along the giant's head. When the giant moved his head quickly for any reason, such as to sneeze, Earth would shake.

■ Some researchers believe that elephants can feel the rumble of seismic activity before people feel it.

Measuring Movement

Scientists use special instruments to measure changes in Earth. One tool is the seismograph. A seismograph measures and records vibrations on the ground and inside Earth.

Seismographs produce wavy lines on paper. These lines record how Earth's crust is moving. Computerized seismographs allow seismologists to track earthquakes to within 6 miles (10 km) of the epicenter.

■ The energy released from a big earthquake is the same as millions of explosives being set off at the same time.

Distance affects energy inside Earth. When objects are close to shock waves, the energy has more effect on the objects. Shock waves have less effect on objects farther away. There are many environmental dangers that occur near the epicenter after an earthquake, including landslides, tsunamis, and fires. Scientists research to find out where major earthquake damage might occur. Then, they make maps to show where dangerous areas might be.

What is a Seismologist?

Seismologists are scientists who study earthquakes. They research Earth's seismic activity. Seismologists look for the cause, kind, and size of seismic activity. They predict where earthquakes may occur.

Computers are useful tools to seismologists. Computers record and **mimic** Earth's movements. Rock movement can be measured using laser beams. Strainmeters measure tectonic plate activity. Strainmeters use laser beams to record the tiniest movements inside Earth.

Beno Gutenberg

Beno Gutenberg was a seismologist who worked as a professor at the California Institute of Technology. He worked with Charles Richter. Gutenberg's research focused on calculating the intensity of different earthquakes. He wrote many books on the subject.

SAFETY
Some seismologists work in areas where there are many earthquakes. This could be dangerous.

WORKING CONDITIONS
Most seismologists work in labs. Some work in universities or for oil companies.

Seven Facts About Earthquakes

There are approximately 500,000 detectable earthquakes each year, but only 100 will cause damage.

Earthquakes that happen underwater cause tsunamis.

Moonquakes are earthquakes on the Moon. They do not happen as often as earthquakes and have smaller magnitudes.

Tectonic plates move at about the same speed as fingernails grow.

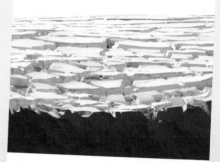

Antarctica has icequakes. Icequakes are like earthquakes but happen inside ice sheets instead of underground.

Most earthquakes happen less than 50 miles (80 km) below the Earth's surface.

Florida and North Dakota are the states with the fewest earthquakes.

Earthquake Brain Teasers

1 On Earth's surface, where are the seismic waves strongest?

2 What is the name of the scale that measures the level of an earthquake?

3 Would a magnitude 3 earthquake cause terrible damage?

4 What is the name for the place where tectonic plates meet?

5 What is the focus?

6 Where do most earthquakes occur?

7 What is the name of the fault line that runs through California?

8 What kind of work do seismologists perform?

9 What can laser beams measure?

10 Which animals did the Gabrielino Indians think held up the Earth?

ANSWERS: 1. The epicenter. 2. The Richter scale. 3. No. 4. A fault line. 5. The underground place where energy is first released during an earthquake. 6. Along the edges of tectonic plates. 7. The San Andreas Fault. 8. Seismologists research earthquakes. 9. Rock movement. 10. Turtles.

Science in Action

Earthquake Fault Model

A fault is a place where there is a break in Earth's crust. You can use clay to make your own model of a fault.

Tools Needed

Three different color of clay

Dull knife

Directions

1 Mold three pieces of clay into rectangles. Make sure each piece is a different color.

2 Each piece of clay represents a different part of Earth's crust. Stack the pieces on top of each other, and push them together.

3 Cut the pieces in half. The cut represents a fault in Earth's crust. Then, put the pieces together. Be sure that the lines do not match up exactly.

4 Push the outsides of the two sections together, and watch how the inside buckles, just like an earthquake.

22

Words to Know

continents: the seven main land masses of Earth—Africa, Antarctica, Asia, Australia, Europe, North America, and South America

crust: Earth's hard, top layer

destruction: great damage or ruin

evacuate: to leave a dangerous area

foundation: the base on which a building stands

magnitude: the size and strength of an earthquake

mimic: act like something else

predict: to say what may happen in the future

seismic waves: bursts of energy that come from the rocks in Earth's crust

tsunami: a powerful wave created when an earthquake occurs on the ocean floor

Index

Log on to www.av2books.com

AV² by Weigl brings you media enhanced books that support active learning. Go to **www.av2books.com**, and enter the special code inside the front cover of this book. You will gain access to enriched and enhanced content that supplements and complements this book. Content includes video, audio, web links, quizzes, a slide show, and activities.

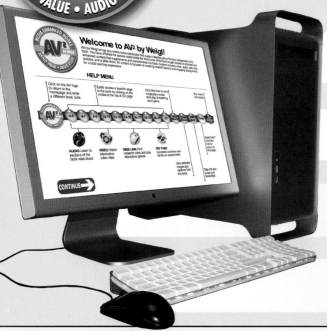

Audio
Listen to sections of
the book read aloud.

Video
Watch informative video clips.

Web Link
Find research sites and
play interactive games.

Try This!
Complete activities and
hands-on experiments.

WHAT'S ONLINE?

Try This! Complete activities and hands-on experiments.	**Web Link** Find research sites and play interactive games.	**Video** Watch informative video clips.	 **EXTRA FEATURES**
Pages 6-7 Complete an activity about earthquakes.	**Pages 8-9** Link to more information about the Richter scale.	**Pages 4-5** Watch a video about earthquakes.	**Audio** Hear introductory audio at the top of every page
Pages 10-11 Use this timeline activity to test your knowledge of world events.	**Pages 16-17** Find out more about earthquake myths.	**Pages 14-15** View a video about a major earthquake.	**Key Words** Study vocabulary, and play a matching word game.
Pages 12-13 See if you can identify earthquakes around the world.	**Pages 18-19** Learn more about being a seismologist.		**Slide Show** View images and captions, and try a writing activity.
Pages 18-19 Write about a day in the life of a seismologist.	**Page 20** Link to facts about earthquakes.		**AV² Quiz** Take this quiz to test your knowledge
Page 22 Try the activity in the book, then play an interactive game.			